# BECKHAM

# BECKHAM

*p*

This is a Parragon Book
First Published in 2004

Parragon, Queen Street House, 4 Queen Street, Bath BA1 1HE, UK

ISBN 1-40543-053-2
Text written by Lucie Cave
Designed by designsection

Printed in Indonesia

# Contents

# 1 footballer

After several months of claim and denial, the traditional accompaniment to any major football transfer deal these days, June 2003 saw David Beckham swap the red shirt of Manchester United for the white shirt of Real Madrid in a deal worth a reported £25 million. The previous 12 years had seen him carve out a career as the most famous footballer on earth.

Born in Leytonstone in London in 1975, David Beckham had always wanted to be a footballer. His dad, Ted, who also dreamed of football glory, was a Manchester United fan and – in the way that dads do – he subtly persuaded his son to follow suit. In fact it was seeing Bryan Robson in action in United's Number 7 shirt that really did it for David and, once hooked, he didn't let go. A report on the BBC's *Blue Peter* about a competition organized by Bobby Charlton's Soccer Coaching School prompted David to apply for a place. Of course he got one and, of course, he won the competition. In fact United legend Bobby Charlton praised the young lad's performance, claiming that David was the most talented 11-year-old he'd seen during the six years his school had been running.

It didn't take long after that for United to approach David and invite him for trials. One thing led to another and on the eve of

his 16th birthday, David Beckham had to make a choice: sign for Tottenham in London or United in faraway Manchester. But it was no choice really, and in 1991 David moved north and signed for United as a trainee.

## First Glory

Things went well at United and his reputation was established quickly. 'From day one, his talent had to be seen to be believed,' said United's youth team coach, Eric Harrison. In true comic book fashion, success on the field came quickly. Though he was not yet a regular in the youth team, which at the time also featured Nicky Butt and Gary Neville, he was called into the side for the FA Youth Cup semi-final against Tottenham in 1992. Victory ensured a meeting with Crystal Palace in a two-legged final. David scored in the first match at Selhurst Park and a 6-3 aggregate win meant that he had won his first trophy and his first winner's medal with United.

The following year saw him make his debut for the first team in a League Cup tie at Brighton, coming on as a second-half substitute. But that was his only appearance of the season. In 1993 he signed professional terms with the club but it was not until December 1994 that he got into the side again. Of course he made

*Far left* The young Beckham was keen on many sports and swam for Chingford High School.

*Left* But it was football that really got him going and early experience of representative football with his local team – Ridgeway Rovers – was good preparation for the future superstar.

*Despite the tensions involved in football David Beckham has always managed to have a laugh during matches.*

the best of it, scoring in a Champions League match against Galatasaray.

In March 1995 Beckham was shocked to be called into the manager's office and told that he was being loaned to Third Division Preston North End for a month. But he didn't moan, he didn't complain, instead he played four games and was made man of the match in three of them. Then, just as suddenly as he left, he was called back to Manchester and made his League debut at Leeds. Looking back, David thinks well of his time at Preston. In fact he comments 'I would say that the month at Preston turned my career around, setting everything off. I needed to be picked up a bit, to be encouraged, and Preston did that for me.'

## The Phenomenon Takes Off

The 1995-96 season saw things go well for Beckham: he played 36 matches, scoring 8 goals, including an FA Cup semi-final winner against Chelsea. United won the Premiership title and the FA Cup and it seemed as if things could hardly get better. But of course they did. In August 1996 the Beckham phenomenon really took off. A few minutes from the end of United's opening league fixture against Wimbledon, Beckham had possession of the ball just inside his own half. He looked up, spotted the Dons' keeper Neil Sullivan off his line, and chipped the ball over his head and into the net from 57 yards – this remains a Premiership record. It was a defining moment for the

*His relaxed attitude to training belies the fact that he works harder than many of his professional colleagues.*

youngster and the start of something bigger than anyone could have predicted.

That autumn he started to score more goals, more spectacular goals, more goals from outside the area. In August, England manager Glenn Hoddle, perhaps seeing something of himself in the young Beckham, called him up for the England squad. On 1 September he made his England debut in a World Cup qualifier against Moldova, which England won 3-0. He kept his place in the England side as they qualified for France 1998. He also played his part as United won the Premiership title for the fourth time in five years. David's second championship medal was accompanied by his winning the PFA Young Player of the Year award.

In 1997-98 Beckham continued to perform for United even though his relationship with Spice Girl Victoria Adams brought all sorts of added pressure into his life. He ended the season as the midfield's leading scorer, though United ended the season without any trophies.

## Down and Up Again

The World Cup in France in 1998 started and ended badly for Beckham. He was dropped from the first match against Tunisia as Glenn Hoddle openly questioned his commitment and his temperament. He came on for the injured

*Beckham in action against Moldova on his debut for the national team in 1996.*

*Right Beckham and Colombian legend Carlos Valderrama swap shirts after their 1998 World Cup clash.*

**Far right** *In 1998 David won the PFA Young Player of the Year award.*

**Opposite** *The ecstasy of success. David Beckham celebrates his first England goal with team-mate Sol Campbell.*

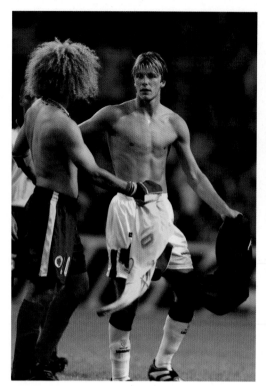

'I have never looked forward to anything in my professional life as much as I did the World Cup finals in France in the summer of 1998.' David Beckham

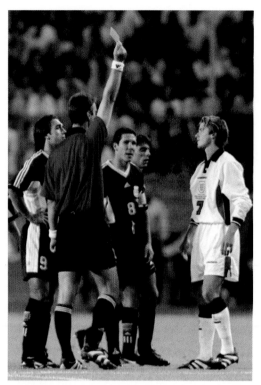

*Right He's off – referee Kim Milton Neilsen sends Beckham off after seeing him kick Argentina's Diego Simeone.*

*Below Public reaction to Beckham's disgrace caused him to think very carefully about his temperament on the pitch.*

Paul Ince in the second match against Romania and then scored his first England goal in the last group game against Colombia to secure a place in the knockout stages. But Beckham and England's tournament ended in shame, as he was sent off just after half-time for aiming a kick at Argentina's Diego Simeone. England finally lost the match on penalties despite a heroic performance and an unforgettable goal by Michael Owen. Hoddle's fears about Beckham's temperament had been justified and many people blamed the young player for England's exit from the tournament.

At the start of the following season, 1998-99, Beckham suffered at the hands of opposition fans who jeered and barracked him constantly, particularly in the early weeks. But for the United fans Beckham had many treats in store that season. His play on the wings and through the middle brought lots of goals for the Andy Cole-Dwight Yorke partnership. So many goals that Manchester United won the Premiership on 16 May, the FA Cup on 22 May and the Champions League on 26 May beating Bayern Munich in the final in Barcelona with two last-minute goals. It was an unprecedented treble, the first time an English club had ever achieved such a thing and as TV commentator Clive Tyldesley commented after the

Bayern game, 'Manchester United have reached the promised land.'

It was a momentous year off the pitch too for David Beckham. On 4 March, Victoria Adams gave birth to their son, Brooklyn, and on 4 July Victoria and David were married in Ireland.

### A True Hero

A poor performance at the European Championships in Belgium and Holland in 2000 and defeat in a World Cup qualifier against Germany soon afterwards saw Kevin Keegan come and go as England manager. Peter Taylor took over the manager's role temporarily while England waited for the arrival from Lazio of new manager Sven-Goran Eriksson. Though Taylor's one match in charge saw a 1-0 defeat against Italy in Rome, it was his decision to make Beckham captain. It was a fine decision and Beckham retains the armband to this day.

Beckham's domestic success continued as United won back-to-back Premiership titles, but it was with England and Sven-Goran Eriksson that he really blossomed. England's form rose under Beckham's leadership. A tremendous 5-1 victory over Germany in Munich in September 2001 was greeted as one of the finest performances ever seen. A month later England met Greece at Old Trafford,

*Above An ever more confident Beckham faces the press with England manager Kevin Keegan.*

*Left A proud Beckham – England captain for the first time – stands for the National Anthem before the game against Italy in November 2000.*

*Above Beckham bends it like… well, Beckham, against Sweden in November 2001.*

*Right Causing hearts to flutter as he removes his shorts during the match with Germany at Wembley in 2001.*

*Far right Looking pleased as he comes second to Luis Figo at the World Player of the Year awards in 2001.*

needing a point for automatic qualification. As a footballer, Beckham has his critics. He flits in and out of matches, he often tries the spectacular instead of doing the simple things, he doesn't score enough goals, he doesn't have enough control of the ball when he dribbles and so on. But that night in Manchester David Beckham played the game of his life. He was everywhere, tackling, passing, running, shooting, geeing up his colleagues. With a minute

'I had quite a few free kicks and was disappointed with most of them. When I got my last chance, Teddy Sheringham said he would have it but I decided I'd take it, it was a good time to score… it was a great feeling.'

David Beckham

or two to go, England were 2-1 down. They got a free kick in Beckham's range and the crowd went quiet with expectation. Beckham ran up to the ball, cheeks puffed out, and struck it cleanly and hard. It arced over the wall and slapped into the back of the net. The crowd went berserk, Beckham ran towards the Stretford End, arms raised, legs wide, it was a moment of true sporting theatre. In that moment, Beckham became a real footballing hero and had, almost single-handedly, got England to Japan and Korea.

*Right* He steps up, cheeks puffed out, and strikes the ball into the Greek goal…

*Far right* …to spark the celebrations of the nation as the captain secures a place in the World Cup finals in Japan and Korea.

*More celebrations after scoring from the spot against old enemy Argentina in Sapporo, Japan, in 2002.*

Though Beckham thrived as England captain, his domestic form was suffering and he was dropped by Sir Alex Ferguson amid stories of a troubled relationship. During this time, it began to be difficult to separate Beckham's footballing career from his celebrity status. When he was injured in a Champions League match against Deportivo in April, it seemed likely that he would not be able to play in the coming World Cup. Of course, this was of concern to readers of the sports section. But pictures of his injured foot also appeared on the front pages and tabloid readers were asked to touch the picture so as to induce some sort of faith healing. Beckham's presence in Japan was essential. Amid unprecedented hysteria and the first real outbreak of 'Beckham-mania', he led England into the competition. Though not on top form, he did enough to slay one particular dragon when he scored the only goal against Argentina from the penalty spot. Revenge for England and for Beckham for 1998 was complete and his importance rose another notch. England's run was ended in the quarter-finals by eventual winners Brazil. At the end of the match, Beckham's face showed the disappointment of the entire nation.

*Becks cannot hide his disappointment after England's quarter-final defeat against Brazil.*

*Beckham signs for Real Madrid with the legendary Alfredo di Stefano (left) and club president Florentino Perez in July 2003.*

**Goodbye Manchester, Hello Madrid**

Beckham's last season at United was a troubled one. His form was patchy as was the team's in general. There were some disappointing results and after one such game, a home defeat against Arsenal in the FA Cup, Sir Alex Ferguson was in a fury. In the midst of his post-match rage he swung his foot at a stray boot which hit Beckham, cutting him on the eyebrow. It was an accident but that did not prevent huge media speculation that things were not well in the United camp. Other stories appeared, particularly from Spain and Italy, in which a number of clubs denied any interest in Beckham. But, of course, there is no smoke without fire. One last hurrah remained. United were drawn against Real Madrid in the Champions League quarter-final. Beckham was not picked for the first leg in Spain, which United lost 3-1. He was not picked for the return match either. However, with United trailing again, Beckham came on and inspired a fantastic fightback. Despite scoring twice and creating a host of other chances United still lost and even more tellingly, Sir Alex Ferguson was captured by the TV cameras dismissing Beckham's efforts with angry gestures. This time the writing truly was on the wall. Though United went on to win the Premiership title again, Beckham's future lay elsewhere and there was no lack of interest in where he was going. Weeks of feverish speculation ended in June when Real Madrid announced that they had signed him.

**Settling In**

Despite the doubters, Beckham started well at his new club, playing well and scoring goals. Three months into his career as a Real Madrid player Beckham

*In joining Madrid, David Beckham has teamed up with some of the finest players in the world. Here he jokes in training with Zinedine Zidane.*

*This page and opposite As a footballer David Beckham has his critics but Real's training regime and his hard work have already bourne fruit with good performances and good results.*

still had a few things to learn about life at the Bernabeu. Real is a unique club, one where ultimate glory only comes with silverware. Regular league or cup victories are hardly celebrated at all. After all, winning is normal for Real. Glory finishes when the match ends. It is said that there is no other team where happiness escapes so quickly. The failure of defeat, however, is remembered until the next game.

Despite this, a victory sees Beckham emerge from the dressing room with a broad grin. He is keen to share his joy

with the press and with his friends. His spectacular goal against Albacete in November, the first in a 2-1 victory that saw Real go to the top of the table for the first time during the season, saw a jubilant Beckham at the press conference. He was typically understated when asked about his stunning 25-yard shot, 'I was pleased with it,' he said. 'It was nice for me to score another one which was not from a set piece.'

He spent much of the rest of the press conference talking about Jonny Wilkinson and England's victory in the rugby World Cup final. Beckham said, 'I spoke to him today – he was just about to go to bed I think. He had just been at another function. He's happy. He's just been so influential in this World Cup for England and every one of the players have just been amazing. I watched the final when I got home from training, which I had taped. I knew the score by then because I had a friend in the crowd and when the trophy was being held up he held his phone up so I could hear the noise. They deserve everything they are going to get because to put in such a performance, and to win the World Cup, you could see what it meant to everyone in England.'

But for now Beckham is taking his life in Spain very seriously. On arrival at the Bernabeu, he was told by Real's Director of Football, Jorge Valdano, that he had to learn Spanish as soon as possible. Valdano was keen that Beckham settle in quickly and that he learned about the particular idiosyncrasies of the club.

Of course, language books were provided and lessons were arranged immediately. Brazilian team-mate Roberto Carlos has also taught Beckham words that he clearly uses during games. Though he is not particularly garrulous on the training ground or in the changing room, Beckham surprised everyone one weekday after training in November when he replied to a question about his fitness from Real's Press Officer Paco Navacerrada: 'Estoy bien,' he said, 'muy bien, puedo jugar perfectamente'. ('I am well, very well, I can play perfectly'.)

*Beckham's England career was enhanced by the appointment of Sven-Goran Eriksson as manager.*

There is no doubt now that Beckham did the right thing in moving to Spain. His fame has brought happiness to Real Madrid and his football has benefited from his new playing colleagues and his new training regime. So central is he to the team that it is almost as though he has played there all his life. With Real heading the Spanish league table and remaining firm favourites for the Champions League and with England ready to play a big part in Euro 2004, there seems no limit to what David Beckham the footballer can achieve in his already successful career.

> 'At the end of the day, it's the family that matters, despite all the success you achieve.' David Beckham

# 2 family man

When asked by *GQ* magazine in May 1999 how he felt about his footballing achievements, Becks said, without hesitation: 'They're important. But having a child means more than anything.'

David Beckham might be the owner of a beautiful face and a super-swift right foot, but to him, all that pales into insignificance compared to the well-being and presence of his family. And it is this unashamed and very public adoration of his wife and kids that endears Becks to us even more. Amazingly, amidst a world of flashbulbs, fans and false rumours he has somehow managed to carve himself a normal family life (even if he does have to fantasize a bit to get there). David explains, 'Sometimes we laugh and call it 'Bubble Beckham': Victoria and I, Brooklyn and Romeo. We're just a family that loves being together, doing what families do. Outside of all that, helping to keep the bubble bouncing along is the fame thing: the attention, the gossip, the paparazzi and the stuff that's just made up.'

Sadly over the past year 'the stuff that's just made up' has tried its best to burst 'Bubble Beckham' once and for all. Even before his transfer to Real Madrid, David had to contend with an attempted kidnap plot on his wife and scurrilous whispers about his personal life spread on the Internet.

*Left Mr and Mrs Beckham share a secret smile while being interviewed for the German TV show* Bet It *in October 2001.*

*Far left Posh, Becks and their matching fringes arrive at London Fashion week to get some inspiration for their next wardrobe at the Berardi show in September 1998.*

No sooner had Becks' boots touched Spanish soil than the rumour-mill switched to overdrive again – alleging that he was seeing 'other women' and that Victoria was refusing to move to Madrid. All this was rubbish of course. And Becks somehow succeeded in rising above the tittle-tattle and emerge more in love with Posh than ever.

From the moment he met her in 1997, David has made it clear he thinks Posh is pretty much as close to perfection as you can get. He famously said, 'I'd love Victoria even if she worked in Tesco,' and ever since tying the knot on their matching thrones in July 1999, he has done everything he can to show he loves her, right down to the smallest detail.

When Victoria modelled for the Maria Grachvogel fashion show in 2000, David made sure she had a massive bunch of flowers waiting for her backstage – illustrating how nothing goes unnoticed. When they're together he fills up her car with petrol so she doesn't have to get her hands dirty. When they're apart they call each other at least 15 times a day. And in the thick of press reports about their marriage crisis last year David showered Victoria with gifts and romanced her with a £625 meal at the Ritz in Madrid – where one waiter commented, 'They were like

*David and Victoria outside Beckingham Palace and very proud of baby son Brooklyn, July 1999.*

young honeymooners in love. I didn't see them let go of each other's hands all night.'

Of course Posh isn't the only important factor in Becks' life. His two little boys mean the world to him and he misses them terribly when he doesn't see them. During the World Cup in Japan in 2002, David ensured he had a video set up in the hotel so he could talk to Victoria face to face and catch a glimpse of Brooklyn tinkering about in his bedroom.

Victoria and David love being parents, and despite punishing work schedules

'We're just a family that loves being together, doing what families do.'

David Beckham

*Brooklyn shows David's fans he's every bit as good on his (Adidas clad) feet as his dad and strides across the pitch clutching David's Premier League championship medal in May 2000.*

*Brooklyn feeds dad a nice cheesy crisp while he's trying to watch United's Premiership match against Bolton Wanderers at Old Trafford, October 2001.*

*Becks shows his son how to watch the game in style as he wears his best suit to support his team against Ipswich, September 2001.*

they take Brooklyn and Romeo with them whenever they can and have never considered a nanny. Before the boys were born, Becks revelled in the prospect of fatherhood (when Victoria was pregnant with Brooklyn she discovered he'd secretly bought a book called *How to be a Daddy*) and since they were born he's been shamelessly physical with his sons – hugging and kissing them at every opportunity. Even David's style relates to Brooklyn and Romeo: he has their names embossed on his football boots, embroidered into the back seat of his TVR sports car and permanently etched

on to his back under the watchful eye of a tattooed guardian angel.

David Beckham has made fatherhood sexy, and family life for him is about sharing the responsibility. 'David changes nappies and is very handy with the vacuum cleaner,' Victoria once boasted. And although the pair led a pampered life with their £2.5 million pad in Sawbridgeworth (aka Beckingham Palace) and more recently their £4.5 million villa *Las Encinas* in Spain, they try to conduct family life as normally as possible. Security at the Beckham family homes is inevitably tighter than a high

*The Beckham family prepare to board a plane to Dubai for a holiday before David heads to Korea for the World Cup in 2002.*

security prison with staff on call 24 hours a day, but that doesn't mean they are waited on hand and foot. While living in England David was often spotted nipping into his local Sainsbury's or Marks and Spencer for some food so he could whip up a lasagne for tea. David and Victoria might be super-celebrities but they don't actually have much of a social life. The only people they like to spend time with, apart from their families, are David's best friend Gary Neville or their mentors Elton John and David Furnish.

But although David prefers to cuddle up with a video than dine at the Ivy, he's by no means a slob. In fact he's meticulously tidy. He cannot relax if there's a speck of dust anywhere. He knows it might seem mad but he can't help it. David is so particular that he arranges objects at right angles, files his shirts in a colour-coded straight line and gets all fidgety unless everything in his fridge is symmetrical (Victoria once said that if there were three cans in the fridge he'd throw away one because of the odd number).

But of course there's nothing wrong with being neat. 'If there's one thing that gets on my nerves it's blokes who leave the seat up,' Victoria moans: 'David has never done that – he's so lovely clean and tidy.'

*Victoria and sons
arrive back in London
after a trip to the
States with dad,
August 2003.*

# 3 style icon

David Beckham might be a warrior on the pitch, but off it he's a plethora of different things. An inherent part of the Beckham phenomenon comes from his amazing ability to change his appearance more often than Christina Aguilera and still look good.

British footballers are not exactly renowned for their sartorial sense (it's either sweaty shorts or sharp suits), but Becks can wear a suit one day and a skirt the next without so much as a second thought.

Becks always tops the best-dressed lists, has been photographed more times than most supermodels and readily admits, 'I'm really glad there's a side to my life rather than just football.'

In fact, David Beckham's flair for fashion is so diverse that university professors have credited him for changing the way men actually think. Dr Andrew Parker from Warwick University concedes, 'He has helped break masculine codes by defying various manly expectations such as what clothes men are allowed to wear.'

Whether dressed in a kaftan, wearing pink nail polish, matching diamond earrings or dubious ruffled shirts – David Beckham has the ability to make women swoon and men want to copy him. As *Heat* magazine rightly said, 'He is one stylish bean.'

*David was already dabbling with the goatee in September 1999.*

## Clothes

Becks made his first impact on the public in 1995 – in a league debut for Manchester United – and although he was obviously good-looking, he was not the most stylish boy on the block (back then, his style comprised sportswear and sponsorship logos). But meeting wife-to-be Victoria Adams in 1997 was a catalytic process that changed his look almost immediately. Going out with a pop star opened up a whole new world of wardrobe possibilities and encouraged by his new lady, David experimented more as his confidence in his looks grew. Understandably, the public perception of Victoria's influence over The Beckham Look™ led to David being the object of a fair few jokes in the media. But in reality, it is Becks, not Posh, who has the ultimate control over his image.

David stresses, 'Victoria has a lot to do with how I look and what I wear. But the final decision is down to me. So the ponytail's my idea. The sarong's my idea.'

*The celebrity couple
bask in the glow of
Posh's pregnancy
with Brooklyn, 1999.*

Indeed, it was this man with the honey highlights who not only purchased the infamous Gaultier wraparound in the Côte d'Azur in the summer of 1998 (he picked it up shopping with Mel B's fiancé Jimmy Gulzar), but also insisted on wearing it to dinner at the Chèvre d'Or restaurant that very evening.

And it was this amazing sight of Mr Beckham in a skirt that gave the British press no choice but to sit up and take notice. Professor Ellis Cashmore from Stafford University says, 'When he appeared in the sarong he was saying *I'm no longer just an ordinary footballer.*'

By 1999 David was a fully-fledged style chameleon. And there was nothing he loved more than coordinating his designer attire with wife Posh – whether it was matching leather catsuits or super-baggy combats (and let's face it, there weren't many footballers who could dress like they were in a boy band and get away with it).

*Right The proud father announces the birth of his son Romeo outside the Portland Hospital, London, September 2002.*

*Far right Making a surreptitious exit from the Ivy, February 2002.*

'David was the inspiration for the Armani cashmere jacket in 2003 and D&G referred to him as their "muse".'

*The name's Beckham, David Beckham. Police sunglasses launch, January 2001.*

## Beckham

*Right* Dressed in a Roberto Cavali kaftan, David chats to Elton John at David Furnish's 40th birthday party, October 2002.

*Opposite* Arriving at the christening of Liz Hurley's baby, (it's a boy, but Becks still decides to wear pink on his nails), July 2002.

In the next few years David flitted easily through the worlds of pirate headscarves, kaftans, open-to-the-navel shirts, ripped jeans and tailored designer suits. Heck, he even looked good in dungarees.

But David has liked his dress sense to startle ever since he was a young boy. 'I do like to be a bit different – I always have,' he admits, 'Once when I was little I was a pageboy. I was shown a couple of outfits and chose one with maroon velvet trousers, which stopped at the knee, long

48

white socks and ballet shoes. My mum said: "You're going to look silly, people will laugh at you," but that was what I wanted to wear. I always take pride in my appearance.'

Under David Beckham's administration, men who previously couldn't tell the difference between D&G and C&A, are now flicking through *Vogue* for style tips. Because he wears it, it must be OK. When David was pictured in a T-shirt bearing the logo of old rockers, The Cult's hit 'Sonic Temple', their record sales rocketed almost overnight. And on one occasion after visiting the Prime Minister at Number 10, he sparked a national debate just for turning up wearing a brown suit. 'The man who made it OK for men to wear skirts, chiffon shirts, top-to-toe leather and nail varnish will soon be responsible for a nation dressed in brown,' wrote the *Evening Standard* the next day.

David Beckham's influence over the fashion world is now so massive that designers themselves cite him as their motivation. It's not so much a case of him following catwalk trends as them following *him*.

Last year newspapers reported that powerhouses D&G and Armani were fighting over the rights to dress him in their spring-summer collections for 2004.

Becks is a natural
when it comes to
posing for the camera.
This ability makes him
attractive to the
manufacturers of all
sorts of products but
particularly those that
promote a certain kind
of 'lifestyle'.

David was the inspiration for the Armani cashmere jacket in 2003 and D&G referred to him as their 'muse' (they even went so far as to hire a troupe of David lookalikes to model one of their catwalk collections). To them, Becks is a billion-dollar mannequin.

David Beckham has also achieved a significant fashion first. In May 2002 he became the first male ever to adorn the cover of a woman's magazine anywhere in the world – on his terms and in his clothes. The magazine in question was *Marie Claire*, and that month it sold 100,000 extra copies.

*Left David debuts his personalized sneakers at England's friendly against Sweden in November 2001.*

*Below David's trainers pay tribute to the importance of the England v Brazil World Cup quarter-final, June 2002.*

51

*David takes his training seriously, but still manages to look stylish while he's doing it.*

But being a style icon isn't always easy. Following his 26th birthday photocall, David was ticked off by the press for wearing a T-shirt featuring a picture of Nazi Adolf Eichmann, and in the summer of 2000 he got into trouble with the anti-smoking lobby for wearing a motorbike jacket bearing a Lucky Strike logo on the back (even though he doesn't smoke himself).

Yet Becks is more than happy to chuckle at himself when it comes to fashion. After Posh joked in a TV interview that he wore her thongs around the house, he good-naturedly responded to the barrage of questions that followed with, 'I don't wear her knickers. It would be a bit worrying if I did because she's a bit smaller than me.'

## Body

Robbie Williams hit the nail on the head when, after being introduced to David Beckham, he said, 'He is devastatingly good-looking. When I first met him I didn't know whether to shake his hand or lick his face.'

And if Robbie had decided to lick his face he wouldn't have been too disappointed. 'David loves to have facials and massages,' revealed Victoria at a press conference in Japan. 'He also likes to get his eyebrows plucked. I am sure there are lots of people who would love

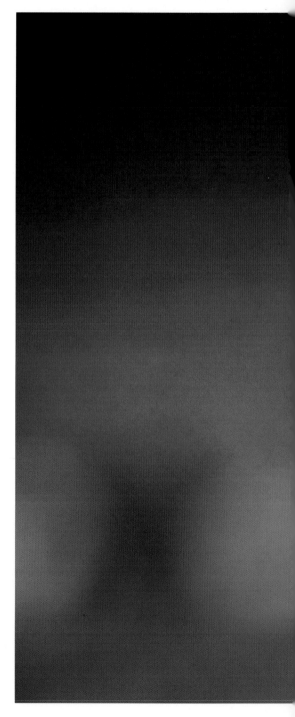

to feel how soft his skin is. His skin is like our baby's.'

Consequently it wasn't long before beauticians in London reported being inundated with bookings from men wanting eyebrow-shaping.

## Jewellery

One of the trends David has nurtured the most is male jewellery, because he's a big lover of bling bling.

Turning up to collect his OBE in November 2003, David's medal was almost overshadowed by the giant sparkler on his finger. Even though he decided not to paint his nails for the Queen, Becks still managed to dazzle for the staff of Buckingham Palace in other ways. Never one to miss an opportunity to shine, he had borrowed a 32-carat diamond ring worth an estimated £5 million for the occasion.

Among Becks' most prized possessions is a glittering £50,000 Franck Muller diamond-encrusted watch which goes with his diamond and gold wedding band and is worth pretty much the same amount. He is also the owner of a £25,000 Theo Fennell cross, matching £5,000 diamond earrings and a £15,000 pinky ring. And just as he was responsible for a nation of new haircuts, experts believe David was responsible for an 11 per cent rise in sales of diamonds in 2002.

*Above With his sparkly studs, polished nails and a hairband, Becks is in danger of outshining the entire launch of his new Pepsi ad, January 2003.*

*Opposite David wows viewers of German TV show* Bet It, *with £70,000 worth of bling bling, October 2001.*

*David is the centre of attention as he takes to Copacabana Beach, Brazil, January 2000, sporting the first of his family tattoos.*

## Tattoos

For most footballers, getting a tattoo goes hand in hand with the job. But when it comes to body art, David Beckham has been typically 'designer' in his selection. His tattoos couldn't be further from the tacky 'I love Mum' variety. Sprawling majestically across his back is a huge open-armed guardian angel (which he designed himself) looking protectively upon the names of his sons Brooklyn and Romeo. His wife is remembered in ink form too: he has the name Victoria inscribed in Hindi on the inside of his left arm to illustrate his love for her (even though one journalist said he'd spelt it wrongly!). And of course he paid tribute to his other love – football – by getting the number seven tattooed in roman numerals on his right arm while playing for Manchester United.

*David's tribute to Victoria is on full display as he prepares for a free-kick in a Champions League match for Real, October 2003.*

*Right* Looking pensive, as he prepares for England's Euro 2004 qualifier against Turkey in Istanbul, October 2003.

*Below* Super-celebrity Becks adjusts his jacket as he arrives at his new Spanish home after signing for Real Madrid, July 2003.

*David and Victoria strolling in the Plaza Oriente, Madrid, September 2003.*

'He is devastatingly good-looking. When I first met him I didn't know whether to shake his hand or lick his face.'

Robbie Williams

'I've had people come in literally the next day with a newspaper saying, "That's what I want."' Hairdresser Trevor Sorbie

*Right Even David's hair wasn't immune to the harsh British weather…*

*Opposite …which is probably why he decided to shave it all off!*

## Hair

David's most famous asset is undoubtedly his barnet. Over the past six years his hairdo has changed more times than Madonna's: from floppy blond locks, to sexy skinhead, American Indian Mohawk, Hoxton fin, messy mullet (complete with Alice band), Bo Derek braids right through to the samurai warrior look.

And Beckham's hairstyles have triggered ferocious tabloid debate. Having finally had enough of his highlights, David reportedly flew his personal hairdresser to Manchester and paid him a whopping £300 to shave it all off. This new number 1 buzz cut was so easy to maintain, that barbers across the country complained about a loss in sales.

*Captain Mohawk of England shows off his symmetrical style at a press conference, May 2001.*

But it wasn't too long before Becks was hatching plans for a new 'do'. And for a couple of months he cunningly walked around in a woolly hat – careful not to let the press see how he'd make his mane grow next. The beginnings of a Mohawk were finally unveiled at a testimonial dinner for his team-mate Ryan Giggs in February 2002. His hair had only grown back slightly, but Becks had still managed to make it dramatically different by means of a zig-zag parting and plenty of gel.

*The Mohican might have cost him a few bob, but there's not one hair out of place.*

63

*A Japanese fan looks pleased with his new Beckham barnet.*

Only David Beckham can have his haircut and guarantee it'll be replicated on the street the following day. When his head was splashed across the front pages sporting a Mohican, hairdresser Trevor Sorbie remarked, 'I've had people come in literally the next day with a newspaper saying, "That's what I want."'

Becks' choice of hairdos doesn't go down well with everyone however. The under-16s football team from Bath's Beechen Hill School were sent home for two days because the headteacher said they looked 'aggressive and yobbish' after having their hair cut in David's image. And when 14-year-old Kenny Jamieson

*Above* Becks pulls his best model face at the launch of the new England away kit, February 2002.

*Left* The Mohawk is moving into mullet territory, May 2002.

*Right* Having roots suddenly becomes sexy as Becks arrives to promote his new range of menswear for Marks & Spencer, September 2002.

*Opposite* Becks ponders whether braids were really such a good idea, South Africa, May 2003.

decided to replicate Becks' braids in 2003, the poor boy was suspended from school.

Although the plaits are placed in Beckham's hair history as his shortest-lived coiffure, they were regarded as a shrewd way of winning over Nelson Mandela. When David took the England team to South Africa in May 2003 his corn-row hair was seen by the African media as an attempt to win local respect.

In fact, they approved of his look so much that they gave it front-page treatment along with artists' impressions of what he might look like with even more ambitious African hairstyles.

But David's tresses aren't just simulated on people's heads. One racy Japanese magazine printed an article encouraging Japanese women to style their private parts the 'Beckham way'.

*He'd look more at home on a surfboard than at the London launch of his autobiography,* My Side, *November 2003.*

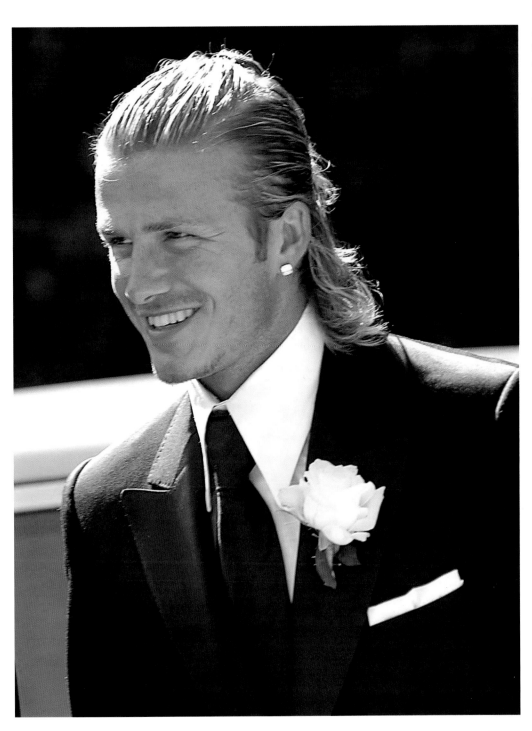

*Becks arrives at the wedding of sporting agent Dave Gardner to Davinia Taylor, July 2003.*

# 'He's not just a football star, not even a superstar, but a global star… admired by everybody.'

## 4 celebrity

Despite having volumes of press written about him, David Beckham remains the ultimate embodiment of celebrity: mysterious, inscrutable and alluring. He is not just a football star, not even a superstar but a global star who is liked and admired by everybody. Grannies remember his face and two-year-olds shout his name when he appears on the TV. 'Beckham' was found to be the most popular computer password in the UK in a nationwide survey of office workers. And in 2001 the National Farmers' Union announced that Becks was among the top five names for cows!

He probably has more lookalikes than any other British celebrity, he is the star of numerous adverts, magazine covers and newspaper column inches and even has a box-office hit movie named after him. David Beckham is a footballer who makes as much news off the pitch as he does on it, a film star who hasn't starred in any movies and royalty who hasn't got a drop of blue blood in his body.

To realize the full power of his star quality – remember that his house in England has been dubbed 'Beckingham' Palace, and that last year one TV programme crowned him 'The most famous black man in Britain.'

*Posh and Becks at their extravagant best in a combo of leather coat and zebra print shoes at a screening of* Withnail and I, *February 2000.*

'... the paparazzi have placed him as number one on their "most wanted" list.'

*The Beckhams adorn a TBC billboard in Japan where they are regarded as the perfect partnership of all time, December 2002.*

University undergraduates can even study him as part of their degree course. David Beckham makes up one module in a Football Culture degree at Staffordshire University where Professor Ellis Cashmore believes, 'Nobody embodies the spirit of our times as well as David Beckham.'

## Most Wanted

There is something so innately fascinating about this good, quiet, unassuming man that the paparazzi have placed him as number one on their 'most wanted' list. Wherever he goes, photographers follow – even though, ironically, most of his movements are actually very unexciting. He rarely goes to showbiz parties, appears at the occasional fashion show, and only steps out for the odd meal with Posh. David says, 'We don't go there [the Ivy] to be flash. When we visit some places we can't eat because people are continually coming up and asking for autographs. We rarely turn down autograph requests but it's nice to finish a meal before it gets cold. In the Ivy they don't let anyone ask for autographs.'

But David's celebrity has not simply emerged because of his marriage to Victoria. She might have initially shown him what it meant to be famous, but over the past six years he's taken it that one step further. By being someone who

*They might not get
hassled inside the Ivy,
but outside it's a very
different story,
October 2003.*

hardly speaks and prefers not to flaunt himself in the public eye, David Beckham has exerted a real grip on the public imagination – and we just can't get enough of him.

## Worldwide Celebrity

We're not the only ones either. David Beckham is a worldwide celebrity. His autobiography became a number one best-seller in China within minutes of hitting the shelves. He is idolized in the Far East and Europe. He has even made headlines in America (where football is almost regarded as a novelty sport).

When David was playing for Manchester United and his team were due to play in the States in the summer of 2003, tickets sold out at staggering speed – 146,000 seats at two matches sold in two hours – which prompted one US newspaper to report that ticket sales were 'quicker than a Bruce Springsteen concert… he's the player even non fans recognize'.

Of course, a celebrity knows they've really made it when they become the subject of comedy. But Britain's Alistair McGowan and Bo! Selecta aren't the only impersonators making money from the Beckham image. Within weeks of signing for Real Madrid, David's celebrity was so well entrenched in Spain that he'd already had a caricature created in his honour.

*Left A fan has his name on her face prior to Real Madrid's match against the China Dragon team, Beijing, August 2003.*

*Below David's Far Eastern fans wear their love for him on their sleeves (OK, arms), August 2003.*

*Opposite Spain's newest resident poses for pictures at the worldwide launch of My Side, the Ritz Hotel, Madrid, September 2003.*

'He was even voted fifth most popular Spaniard by one TV programme!'

*Left* Becks the pop star at the MTV Movie Awards, *Los Angeles, May 2003.*

**Opposite** *The Beckhams at a tennis tournament with other members of the Real Madrid squad, October 2003.*

*Above High-speed police escorts take David to Madrid's La Zarzuela hospital for his world famous medical, July 2003…*

*Opposite …and as usual he's got a few friends waiting to capture his arrival.*

In Spain's answer to *Spitting Image*, Becks was affectionately satirized not for the way he talks, but for his hundreds of hairdos: 'My hair's natural!' his puppet shouted on prime-time Spanish TV.

Just like us, the Spanish love him. According to estimated figures, his Real Madrid number 23 shirts are selling faster than Ronaldo's number 11 the previous year. Women's underwear featuring David Beckham's name is one of the hottest sellers in Spanish clothes shop Zara.

*Right Spanish fans double-check to see what he looks like in case he tries to leave his Madrid hotel in disguise, July 2003.*

*Below left Becks' new number is 23, and his shirts have sold like hot cakes.*

*Below right Chinese fans go wild with delight as David signs his new team's shirts, Beijing, August 2003.*

At the end of last year a Spanish museum, the Museo de Cera, announced plans to build a Beckham waxwork. He was even voted fifth most popular Spaniard by one TV programme!

Yet somehow, despite this adulation and the never-ending attention, David Beckham has remained cool and self-effacing, refusing to become a victim of his own success.

*Just like the sun in Spain, David never stops smiling, July 2003.*

# 'David Beckham has fast become the most… marketable man on the planet.'

## 5 model

Because of his capacity to be all things to all people, David Beckham has been recognized as having the ability to sell anything to anyone. Not only does he have a pretty face and a toned torso, he has an untarnished and scandal-free reputation (something relatively rare in footballers), the ideal family life, he doesn't drink much or smoke, and is adored by women and children, straight and gay people. It doesn't take a genius to work out – this makes him a marketing executive's dream.

David has become one of the most desired promotional tools in the world. Whether it's modelling clothes and sunglasses, or selling chocolate and second-hand cars, the Beckham brand is big business. It's not only in Britain either. David Beckham's fan base in Europe and the Far East is phenomenal, and now even American businesses are starting to sit up and take notice of a footballing hero whose appeal is so great he could stop playing football now and still be adored.

### Lucrative Endorsement Deals

As the adulation for Becks has rolled in, so have the lucrative endorsement deals. With his sculpted good looks he rakes in just as much in sponsorships as he does playing football.

*Surveys have proved that Becks' involvement with Castrol Oil has increased sales in Vietnam and Thailand.*

*Surveys have proved that Becks' involvement with Castrol Oil has increased sales in Vietnam and Thailand.*

David Beckham has fast become the most desired, photographed and marketable man on the planet. Over the last two years he has earned over £30 million for promoting products like Castrol, Brylcreem, Pepsi, Vodafone, Police sunglasses, Rage software, Marks & Spencer and Adidas.

His recent whistle-stop tour of the Far East is reported to have earned him a further £16 million in 10 days. If the British love David Beckham, the Japanese adore him. Set foot in the Far East and it's more than likely you'll be faced with a life-sized poster of Mr Beckham round every corner. His fans will buy into anything he puts his name to – whether he's extolling the virtues of chocolate-covered almonds, face cream or sushi. A survey in Thailand, Vietnam and China even revealed that 80 per cent of consumers felt a link with David Beckham

*Left* David and Victoria are seen as the embodiment of perfect family life in posters across the Far East.

*Below* Perhaps the Tokyo Beauty Centre should change its name to the Beckham Centre instead…

*Overleaf* David leaves other supermodels in the shade as he smoulders for a Police advertising campaign, February 2002.

'Whether it's modelling clothes and sunglasses, or selling chocolate and second-hand cars, the Beckham brand is big business.'

*David was immortalized as a computer programme for the Gameboy Advance and Sony Playstation soccer game, October 2001.*

'His whistle-stop tour of the Far East is reported to have earned him £16 million in 10 days.'

ダイエット ベッカム。

*Drink, David? Becks poses for a Japanese ad for Pepsi, August 2003.*

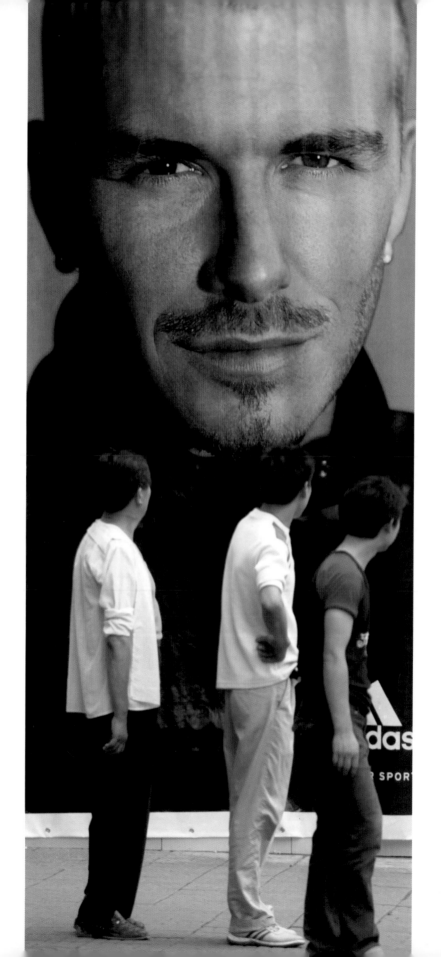

would be a positive reason to buy Castrol oil. And such is the power of Becks that even his contract-clinching medical in Madrid last year was sponsored by a health-care firm.

## The Face of Football

One of David Beckham's first assignments was modelling the England football kit to the British press. He became the face of football, and his chiselled jaw was quickly recognized as being in a very different category to the likes of David Seaman and Alan Shearer.

Because of this, David Beckham became the first footballer ever to receive image rights (payment for the earning potential his image provided his club). While playing for Manchester United he was collecting a wage of approximately £70,000 per week plus £20,000 per week for the club to use his image.

Part of his contract with Real Madrid means they own his image rights (he has to pay them 50 per cent of whatever he earns outside football) but it is estimated that his future deals will be on a much bigger global scale and therefore much more lucrative. Luckily for Becks, his personal contract to promote Pepsi worked well with Manchester United and now Real Madrid because Pepsi is the official sponsor of both teams. And

*Left* The perfect face for football. Becks launches the England Umbro kit, January 2001.

*Opposite* Even grown men can't keep their eyes off him as they pass his picture in China, July 2003.

although Nike sponsors United, Becks managed to strike a personal deal with Adidas to wear their Predator boots while he was still playing for them.

Becks' move to Spain was understandably called a 'dream ticket' by Adidas boss Herbert Hainer, because they sponsor the whole of Real Madrid. And he was rewarded accordingly in August 2003 when he made the biggest commercial deal in football history – signing to Adidas bootmakers for life in return for a package worth up to £100 million.

Another big brand synonymous with David Beckham is Vodafone. Because they also sponsor Manchester United, his

Beckham

*A Chinese lady sits aboard the Beckham bus, Shanghai, August 2001.*

'His clever lawyers have already registered his name for products like perfume, deodorants, jewellery, purses, dolls and football tops.'

*David and Juan Sebastian Veron pose for photographers at the launch of a new Pepsi advert, January 2003.*

*A waxwork version of Becks makes shopping that little bit more pleasant for people in a Japanese department store.*

individual contract with them worked well. However, moving to Siemens-sponsored Real Madrid could well have caused him more than a few headaches. But fortunately the Siemens handset works well with the Vodafone network so David manages to represent both brands with no trouble. And because Becks never appears in Vodaphone adverts in his football kit he doesn't offend rival clubs, appearing instead as a powerful lifestyle icon.

### The 'Meterosexual'

It is here, as a lifestyle icon, that experts say his future lies once he has hung up his boots. Economists are already referring to him as 'meterosexual': 'a heterosexual urban male who enjoys fashion and grooming products, and even activities such as parenting that are traditionally associated with women'.

Last year David Beckham signed a new management deal, with *Pop Idol* guru (and Victoria's manager) Simon Fuller. Fuller

A Japanese commuter stares approvingly as she passes an advertising image on the Tokyo subway, December 2002.

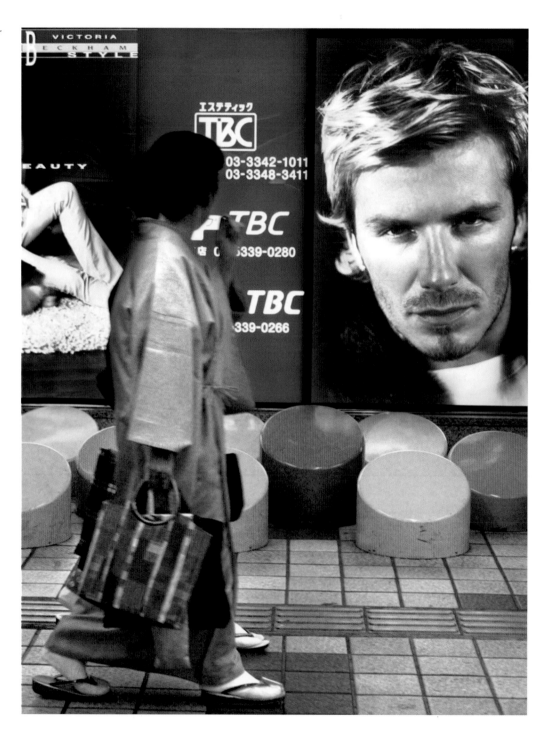

has since announced his post-football plans to turn David into an international icon of masculinity and fatherhood.

David Beckham is a superbrand that just keeps growing and growing. His clever lawyers have already registered his name for products like perfume, deodorants, jewellery, purses, dolls and football tops.

David Beckham looks set to become bigger than Bart Simpson. Real Madrid were quick to recognize his massive commercial pull and began talks with Disney to create 'Superhero Becks' more or less immediately after signing him in July. If it goes ahead, the cartoon will be called *Allstar Striker* and will be sold to more than 150 countries worldwide.

*A man reads the Chinese version of Becks' autobiography, unaware that he's leaning on the author himself, November 2003.*

# 'He moved the crowd to tears as he gave the Jubilee baton to Kirsty.'

## 6 humanitarian

One of the most overwhelming and underrated of David Beckham's qualities is his intrinsic desire to help others. Whether it's something as simple as a smile or as life-changing as charity work, David has the ability to make people feel special. For someone who causes mass hysteria wherever he goes, he is remarkably modest and humble. He might be a superstar, but he certainly doesn't act like one. Whoever he meets – whether it's the Queen, a homeless person or a sick child – he treats them with a genuine warmth and affection.

It is this kindness and humility that led to David Beckham topping a poll last year as Britain's Mr Compassionate. But ironically, this is the very thing he'd prefer not to be acknowledged for. Unlike some celebrity couples, David and Victoria are not well known for their charity work – but that doesn't mean they don't help others. They just refuse to use other people's misfortunes as a way of getting credit for themselves.

When David was playing for Manchester United he and Victoria were regular visitors to various hospitals where they spent time donating and handing out presents to sick children. Friend Frank Lammar comments, 'They did this completely from the heart and not for personal publicity. The majority of these

*Above Becks poses with one of his fans, Bangkok, July 2003.*

*Opposite David wishes he had more hands at a Tokyo school, June 2003.*

visits attracted no press coverage whatsoever and this is the way they wanted it to be.'

### Treasured Causes

For one particular 7-year-old, a visit from David Beckham was the best present he could wish for. Dean Cooper, from Barmall, spent much of his young life in hospital fighting a series of blood disorders, and was asleep in the Royal Manchester hospital when David arrived. When he woke to see his hero sitting at his bedside he beamed from ear to ear. Dean's dad Dennis Cooper said, 'I'm not ashamed to say I cried my eyes out afterwards. Poor Dean has not had a lot to smile about for a long time, but he absolutely idolizes David Beckham. David was wonderful. Dean has not stopped smiling since.'

One of David's most treasured causes has been that of young Kirsty Howard. The terminally ill girl with a rare heart condition moved Becks to tears when he first met her. Becks held her hand as she walked on to the pitch at Old Trafford acting as mascot for the national team in the World Cup qualifier against Greece in 2001. And he remembers, 'In my memory, meeting Kirsty at the start of the afternoon is up there with scoring my goal at the end of it.' Kirsty's dad Steve recalls, 'He was fantastic with her – he kept talking to her, stroking her head, making sure she was OK with all the noise and crowds. You could see something special was going on. Despite all the responsibility on his shoulders he was looking after Kirsty. He made sure

'David's ability to relate to kids is special... he regards them as his equals.'

the whole team – Greeks too – all said hello as if she was the most important person there.'

Becks has helped raise money and awareness for Kirsty's charity, the Francis House Hospice in Manchester ever since. Later, at the Commonwealth Games Ceremony, dressed in his famous white and gold tracksuit, he moved the crowd to tears as he gave the baton to Kirsty who handed it to the Queen.

*David meets a fan in Kuala Lumpur in June 2003 as he arrives for a one-day visit as part of his Asian tour.*

*Braided Becks poses*
*with school kids at*
*Nelson Mandela's*
*foundation office*
*in Johannesburg,*
*May 2003.*

### Special Ability

David's ability to relate to kids is special. Because no matter how young they are, he regards them as his equals. One example of this is when David was greeting the world's media, having just signed to Real. A Spanish fan broke on to the pitch and started running towards him. Rather than panicking and allowing security guards to drag him away, David's instinct was to hold his arms out, hug him tightly and present him with a Real football shirt. David smiles, 'He looked up at me, his eyes were like a mirror: happiness, fear, awe, the wonder of the impossible just having happened.'

*This page and opposite David makes a young Spanish boy's dreams come true when he ran, uninvited on to the pitch at Real Madrid's training ground, July 2002. And he got a new shirt into the bargain.*

*Becks carries a reluctant mascot on to the pitch with him before the Euro 2004 qualifier against Liechtenstein at Old Trafford, September 2003.*

*After a training session in Hong Kong, loving Becks shakes hands with orphan children who lost their parents to SARS, August 2003.*

Little Keilsha Hayward got similar treatment in 2002 when she burst into tears on the pitch at Old Trafford because the task of being the mascot for Manchester United's game against Everton was too much for her. Women across Britain melted as they watched Becks put aside his role as professional footballer and immediately rush over to comfort her with reassuring words.

Of course, it isn't just youngsters on the receiving end of David's good nature. There are numerous examples of his humility and gratitude in everyday situations. From calling for a breakdown truck to help a stranded motorist, to personally telephoning to thank a shop assistant who'd handed his lost wallet in to the police. David Beckham is a first class humanitarian.

# 7 public figure

The extent of David Beckham's influence on the public is such that in a recent poll he was voted more popular as an icon than Elvis or Martin Luther King – more trusted by people than the Prime Minister. He might not be a natural leader, but over the past few years David Beckham has developed and matured in the public eye to such an extent that he is now regarded as one of the most influential and respected figures in Britain. Becks is no orator but he is very smart.

## The Transformation

David Beckham has transformed himself from the most vilified man in Britain to the most beloved. He has blossomed from the boy who was too shy to speak to a Spice Girl into a man for whom meeting the Queen, chatting to the Prime Minister and conversing with world leaders is now second nature. He is captain of the England football team and, according to Spanish paper *El Mundo*, could also 'be Madrid's captain, in time'. Becks' positive public image has largely emerged from the fact that he is a 'bad boy done good'. Before being sent off in the 1998 World Cup against Argentina – David was seen as a *nouveau* celebrity who was easy to mock. But faced with genuine adversity

*David and Sir Alex Ferguson are all smiles after receiving their trophies at the BBC's Sports Personality of the Year, December 2001.*

as captain. He turns a lot of negatives into positives and you can really look up to him as a role model.'

This sentiment was echoed when David was voted Sports Personality of the Year in 2001. At the end of the programme as the credits rolled, Becks stood overwhelmed by emotion, his eyes welling up with tears.

### Highly Motivated to Succeed

The drive and obsessive personal focus that David Beckham applies to his football is reflected in all other areas of his life. He is highly motivated to succeed in whatever he's doing.

In November 2003, the Queen formally acknowledged David Beckham's achievements when he received an OBE in recognition of his services to the sport he's devoted his life to and as a positive role model to the millions of children who look up to him. He arrived at Buckingham Palace dressed in a traditional top hat and tails, wowing both the media and the Queen with his humble charm. He said, 'Her Majesty said she was very pleased to be giving me this award. I know she's a football fan because when I was at a Number 10 reception the Prime Minister told me he had watched a World Cup game on television with the Queen, William and Harry!'

and public hatred, David Beckham showed real steel. Rather than trying to make excuses, he gritted his teeth, carried on and with sheer determination managed to turn his fortunes around to the extent that he was asked to be England's captain. David admits, 'I could've done interview after interview explaining myself and talking my way round it. But I've just gone out there and worked hard to get where I am today.'

England team-mate Rio Ferdinand agrees, 'David Beckham has been brilliant

*David and Victoria look the part as they arrive at the real Buckingham Palace where David was presented with his OBE by Her Majesty the Queen, November 2003.*

*Above David meets Nelson Mandela and proudly presents him with his own shirt, May 2003.*

*Above right David meets Her Majesty the Queen during a reception for the FA held at Buckingham Palace, November 2002.*

One of David's most high profile and significant meetings was with Nelson Mandela in the summer of 2003. The England team were due to play a match against South Africa the following day. But despite the fact that the Football Association insisted the Mandela visit was voluntary (as it was a long flight away from where the game was to be played), David insisted on getting up early and travelling to meet him. Becks appeared genuinely awe-struck to be in the company of the 84-year-old living legend – telling people afterwards he was 'inspirational' and a 'father figure'. Complete with corn-row hair, David

greeted him with a maturity and dignity that illustrated just how important he felt this moment to be. 'As England captain,' he said with a falter, 'I'd just like to say it's a great honour for me, the manager, the FA and the rest of the players to be here today. To meet a great man such as you is a great honour for anyone involved.' In a gesture of respect and admiration recognized throughout the world of sport, David then added, 'We have a shirt for you.'

But significantly, the perception of David Beckham was such, that in the eyes of some of the British public, he even surpassed this historical figure in greatness. One

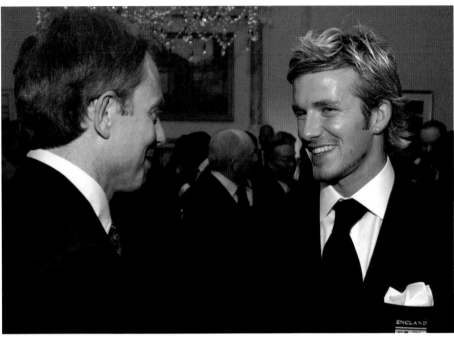

newspaper summed it up beautifully with the headline, 'A household name and adored by his nation. Aren't you lucky to meet him, Mr Mandela?'

### Good Manners

Becks' role as England captain has meant he's been a regular visitor to Number 10. Tony Blair even sent him a get-well message when he injured his foot in the run-up to the 2002 World Cup. This superstar footballer has also tentatively entered the world of politics by getting involved in the euro debate. Speaking from his new home in Madrid he gave his approval of the euro: 'I've had to get used to a few things in Spain and the euro is one of them. Of course, I'm used to it now. It's really easy and it's not a problem.'

For someone who, for a good part of his adult life has been teased for having a girly speaking voice, David has also become a confident public speaker. He says, 'I've become used to public speaking since I got the England armband,' and laughs, 'in fact Victoria reckons the difficult bit is getting me to stop making speeches.'

Well aware that his voice is his Achilles heel, David is more than happy to laugh about it. And in doing so he wins over an army of new fans each time. At one of his

*Above Becks meets Tony Blair at a Number 10 party to celebrate England's performance in the 2002 World Cup.*

*Ponytailed to perfection, David arrives in Skopje, Macedonia before England's World Cup qualifier, September 2003.*

first press conferences in Madrid, he joked about getting to grips with a new language saying, 'It took me 28 years to learn English!'

David's sense of humour is one of the things that makes him so captivating. In the ITV documentary *The Real David Beckham*, David and Victoria were filmed on their way to the infamous interview with Michael Parkinson and he grinned, 'He's bound to use a couple of long words I don't know.' In reality, of course, it wasn't the long words David needed to worry about. And when Posh accidentally told Parky her husband's nickname was 'Goldenballs' – he simply mock grimaced and took it all in his stride.

David's reach is so great that he and Victoria were guests of honour at the 50th anniversary bash to celebrate the discovery of DNA in an attempt to make science more popular.

But it's not just what David Beckham puts his name to that makes him such a strong public figure. He has been credited by academics with single-handedly transforming male behaviour and attitudes on a global scale. Becks has helped transform attitudes to love, sex, babies and homosexuality.

And despite the enormity of his fame – David Beckham is a public figure with manners your granny would be proud of.

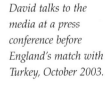

*Clockwise from top left Becks is in the spotlight as he arrives on stage to be presented with his new team shirt in Madrid, July 2003.*

*A Chinese girl squeezes in amongst the paparazzi while trying to catch a glimpse of her hero as she waits for him to arrive for a training session in Kunming, July 2003.*

*Becks is all smiles as he faces the press before his home debut for Real Madrid, August 2003.*

*David talks to the media at a press conference before England's match with Turkey, October 2003.*

> '**Only David Beckham can fracture his foot and have the Prime Minister make a speech about it.**'

# 8 hero

David Beckham is adored. He is idolized. He is worshipped. He has transcended celebrity, sport and superstardom to become an iconic embodiment of the spirit of our time. To put it into perspective, Princess Diana's funeral received the highest TV viewing figures ever – the signing of Beckham for Real Madrid received the second highest.

There's something very exciting about David Beckham that people react to, he generates hysteria wherever he goes. His effect is such that he somehow unites people in a form of communal worship. His appeal crosses boundaries. He is as much a star for football-haters as for football-lovers, for poor as for rich and for black as for white.

Of the world's sporting superstars only David Beckham has a Buddhist statue built in his honour. Only David Beckham can draw crowds of over 35,000 just to watch him train in Tokyo. Only David Beckham can fracture his foot and have the Prime Minister make a speech about it.

### Worldwide Worship

Shortly after 8 p.m. on Wednesday 18 March 2002, David Beckham hurt his left foot in a match against Deportivo La

*Above South African fans welcome their hero, May 2003.*

*Top right A Japanese girl waits for a glimpse of her idol, Awaji Island, Japan 2002.*

*Bottom right Victory against Argentina in the World Cup is greeted with delight in a North London pub, June 2002.*

Coruña, throwing his potential to take part in the World Cup finals into doubt. By lunchtime the following day, news about that injury occupied eight solid pages on the BBC's Ceefax service – seven more pages than were devoted to any other story (including the Queen Mother's death 11 days before). The *Sun* newspaper printed a replica of his bare foot on the cover, begging its readers to use it as a prayer mat and 'rub it at noon and pray'. And tourists flocked to David's waxwork at Madame Tussaud's to rub his foot and surround it with well-wishing flowers.

Of course, David Beckham is not just a national hero. His worship is worldwide. During the 2002 World Cup he was treated to a pop star reception and thousands of camera flashes went off around Tokyo's stadium every time he took a corner kick. Since then, people regularly pay thousands of pounds per night to stay in the same hotel room that he slept in between games.

*Becks waves to fans after England's momentous win against Argentina during the World Cup, Sapporo, June 2002.*

*Chinese fans play 'Who has the biggest poster of Becks?' at a Real Madrid training session, Beijing Stadium, August 2003.*

During his whirlwind 10-day tour of the Far East in 2003, David Beckham experienced nothing short of Beatlemania when he landed at Tokyo airport with his wife Victoria. The couple were greeted by over a thousand screaming Japanese girls who'd turned up at the airport to meet them. Later on the same trip they visited what was described as 'a secluded beach' in Bangkok to film a TV advert, but over a hundred fans were already there waiting to catch a glimpse of them. And when David broke his right wrist, Japanese party-goers went to nightclubs wearing casts on their arms in his honour. This worship knows no bounds.

*Real Madrid's Far Eastern tour in August 2003 saw scenes of mass hysteria reminiscent of 'Beatlemania'. Thousands of fans greeted him at the airports and thousands more bought tickets proving that David Beckham has fans all over the world.*

*Right Buddhist Becks: a statue of David stands in Bangkok's Pariwas temple for fans to worship.*

*Opposite 2003 saw David Beckham's popularity rise to unprecedented proportions. Success at his new club will ensure that he remains one of the most famous people on the planet.*

'He has transcended celebrity, sport and superstardom to become an iconic embodiment of the spirit of our time.'

### Beckham the Deity

Ever since 2000 David Beckham can be found immortalized in gold leaf as a Buddhist statue in Bangkok in Thailand. His effigy stands a foot high alongside gods and Thai historical figures in the city's Pariwas temple. The temple's senior monk, Chan Theerapunyo, said, 'We have to open our minds and share the feelings of millions of people who admire Beckham.'

David Beckham is the only British icon to be portrayed as both Jesus and a Hindu deity. In February 2002, artists Amrit and Rabindra Singh painted David Beckham as the Hindu god Shiva, his wife Victoria as the goddess Parvati and even Brooklyn appeared as the elephant god Ganesh. So revered is he that you could almost be forgiven for thinking that the worship of David Beckham is the new religion.

# Acknowledgements

## ABOUT THE AUTHOR

Lucie Cave is a journalist and TV presenter. She is currently deputy news editor at *Heat Magazine*, where she feeds her thirst for all things celebrity (which includes keeping a beady eye on David Beckham's every move). She also writes a gossip column for *J17*, is a showbiz reporter for Trouble TV, and has appeared on a number of shows for Channel 4, Sky One and Channel 5. In 2003, Lucie wrote the unofficial Busted annual for Contender, this is her second book.

## FOR DESIGNSECTION

Additional text and editorial: Julian Flanders
Design: Rhiannon Sully and Carole McDonald

## PICTURE CREDITS

Parragon would like to thank the following for providing photographs and for permission to reproduce copyright material. While every effort has been made to trace and acknowledge all copyright holders, we would like to apologize should there have been any errors or omissions.

**Empics:** endpapers, 10, 11, 12, 14 (right), 16, 17, 18, 19, 21, 22, 23, 30, 35, 37, 42, 51, 52, 61, 64, 65 (left), 70, 75, 89, 94, 95, 112, 120, 122 (left); **Reuters:** 2 (top left, bottom left), 6, 14 (left), 15, 20, 24, 25, 26, 27, 28, 29, 32, 33, 36, 38, 40, 44, 54, 55, 58, 62, 63, 66, 67, 68, 72, 78, 79, 80, 82, 83, 84 (top, bottom right), 85, 86, 90, 96, 98, 99, 100, 101, 102, 104, 105, 106, 107, 108, 109, 110, 111, 115, 116, 117, 118, 119, 122 (top right, bottom right), 123, 124, 125, 126, 127, 128; **Rex Features:** cover, 2 (top right, bottom right), 3, 8, 9, 34, 39, 43, 46, 47, 48, 49, 50, 56, 57, 59, 60, 65 (right), 69, 74, 76, 81, 84 (bottom left), 88, 92, 93, 114; **The Sun:** 45